ideals®

COUNTRYSIDE

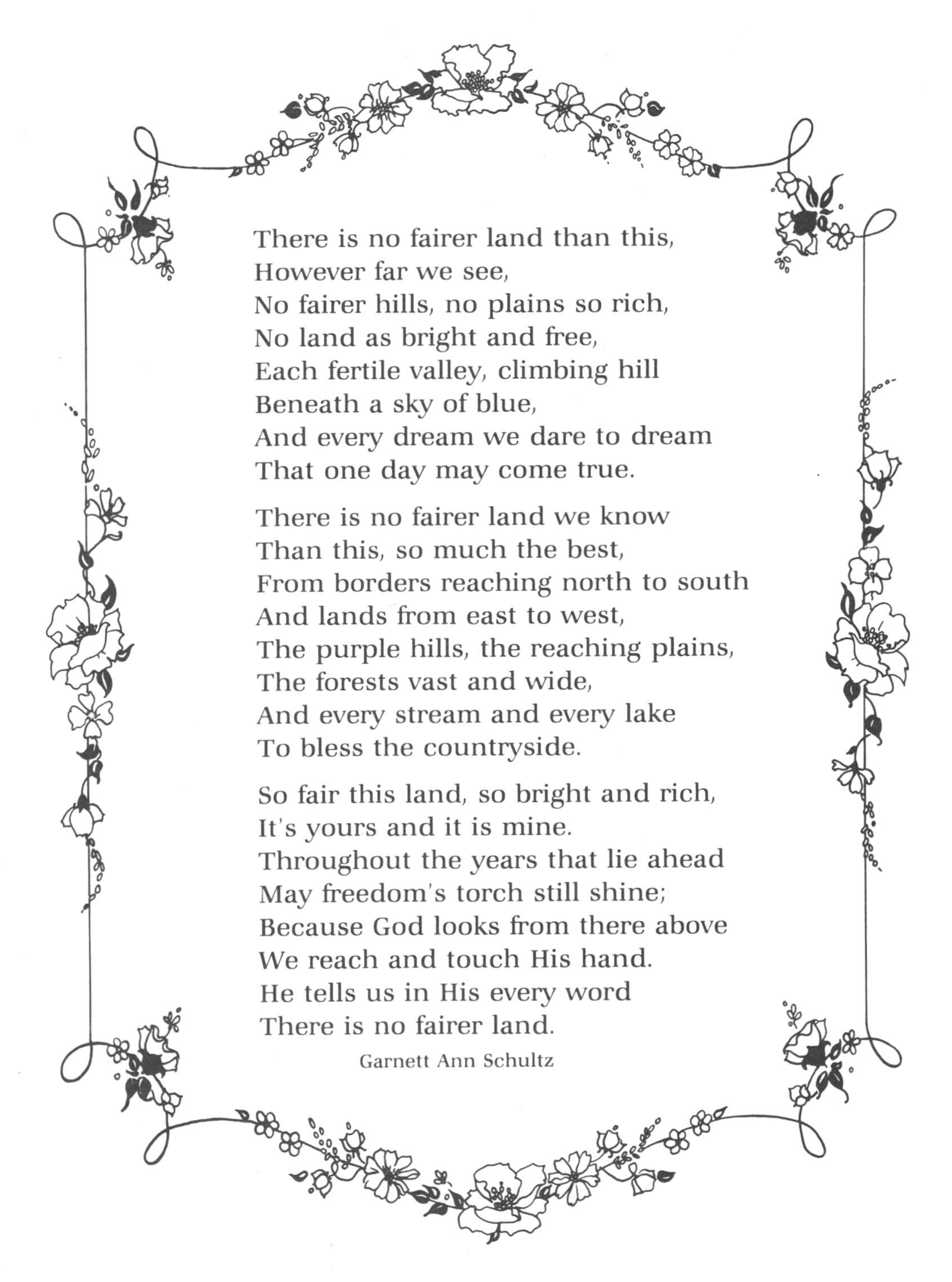

There is no fairer land than this,
However far we see,
No fairer hills, no plains so rich,
No land as bright and free,
Each fertile valley, climbing hill
Beneath a sky of blue,
And every dream we dare to dream
That one day may come true.

There is no fairer land we know
Than this, so much the best,
From borders reaching north to south
And lands from east to west,
The purple hills, the reaching plains,
The forests vast and wide,
And every stream and every lake
To bless the countryside.

So fair this land, so bright and rich,
It's yours and it is mine.
Throughout the years that lie ahead
May freedom's torch still shine;
Because God looks from there above
We reach and touch His hand.
He tells us in His every word
There is no fairer land.

Garnett Ann Schultz

ISBN 0-8249-1012-5 350

IDEALS—Vol. 39, No. 5 August MCMLXXXII IDEALS (ISSN 0019-137X) is published eight times a year,
February, March, April, June, August, September, November, December
by IDEALS PUBLISHING CORPORATION, 11315 Watertown Plank Road, Milwaukee, Wis. 53226
Second class postage paid at Milwaukee, Wisconsin.
POSTMASTER: Send address changes to Ideals, Post Office Box 2100, Milwaukee, Wis. 53201

Published simultaneously in Canada.

ONE YEAR SUBSCRIPTION—eight consecutive issues as published—$15.95
TWO YEAR SUBSCRIPTION—sixteen consecutive issues as published—$27.95
SINGLE ISSUE—$3.50

July

The year is half o'er when enters July,
Demure in her manner, sweet, gracious, and shy;
Casting bright, mellow warmth over mountain and rill
And the last rose of summer that's lingering still.
There is no fairer day nor more radiant sky
Than is found in the keeping of blissful July!

For it's then that the daisies and buttercups bloom;
Then songbirds sing best, and the world is in tune.
The air then is balmiest; trees are the greenest;
Flowers are prettiest, and life is serenest.
Then together midyear and midsummer pass by.
O lackadaisical, soulful July!

And in the mild evening her smooth gentle breeze
Whispers soft lullabies through the green trees,
While her star-studded sky and dreamy old moon
Invite competition with hazical June.
And the meadow is lit by the wild firefly.
What month has more splendors than gorgeous July?

Ruth Hathaway Miller

Ideals' Best-Loved Poets

William Wordsworth

Often acclaimed for his descriptions of nature, the English poet William Wordsworth was born April 7, 1770, in Cumberland. Both of his parents died when he was a boy, and he was left in the care of relatives. When he was seventeen, he entered Cambridge University, taking with him a love of composing verse. Upon graduation in 1791, Wordsworth traveled to France where he became sympathetic to the French Revolution. He returned home the next year and roamed the English countryside. Wordsworth met Samuel Taylor Coleridge in 1796, and within three years the two poets had compiled LYRICAL BALLADS, containing a majority of Wordsworth's writings including the famed "Tintern Abbey." Many scholars consider this the beginning of the romantic movement in England. In his lyrics, Wordsworth wrote more freely than the traditional poets, asserting that serious poems could portray "situations from common life" and could be written in the language "really used by men." In 1802, Wordsworth married Mary Hutchinson, and they had five children. He continued to write poetry throughout his lifetime, including many sonnets. In his sonnets, Wordsworth expressed what he considered to be the three great subjects of poetry: man, nature, and human life. Queen Victoria bestowed upon him the honor of poet laureate in 1843. Wordsworth died April 23, 1850. Through his writings, readers are enabled to regard life itself with new eyes.

To a Skylark

Ethereal minstrel! pilgrim of the sky!
Dost thou despise the earth where cares abound,
Or while the wings aspire, are heart and eye
Both with thy nest upon the dewy ground?
Thy nest which thou canst drop into at will,
Those quivering wings composed, that music still!

To the last point of vision, and beyond,
Mount, daring warbler! That love-prompted strain—
Twixt thee and thine a never-failing bond—
Thrills not the less the bosom of the plain,
Yet might'st thou seem, proud privilege, to sing
All independent of the leafy spring.

Leave to the nightingale her shady wood;
A privacy of glorious light is thine,
Whence thou dost pour upon the world a flood
Of harmony with instinct more divine:
Type of the wise who soar but never roam,
True to the kindred points of heaven and home!

From Tintern Abbey

For I have learned
To look on nature, not as in the hour
Of thoughtless youth but hearing oftentimes
The still, sad music of humanity,
Nor harsh nor grating though of ample power
To chasten and subdue. And I have felt
A presence that disturbs me with the joy
Of elevated thoughts: a sense sublime
Of something far more deeply interfused
Whose dwelling is the light of setting suns
And the round ocean and the living air
And the blue sky and in the mind of man,
A motion and a spirit that impels
All thinking things, all objects of all thought,
And rolls through all things. Therefore am I still
A lover of the meadows and the woods
And mountains and of all that we behold
From this green earth, of all the mighty world
Of eye and ear—both what they half create
And what perceive—well pleased to recognize
In nature and the language of the sense,
The anchor of my purest thoughts, the nurse,
The guide, the guardian of my heart, and soul
Of all my moral being.

The Daffodils

I wandered lonely as a cloud
That floats on high o'er vales and hills,
When all at once I saw a crowd,
A host of golden daffodils
Beside the lake, beside the trees,
Fluttering and dancing in the breeze.

Continuous as the stars that shine
And twinkle on the Milky Way,
They stretched in never-ending line
Along the margin of a bay;
Ten thousand saw I at a glance,
Tossing their heads in sprightly dance.

The waves beside them danced, but they
Outdid the sparkling waves in glee;
A poet could not but be gay
In such a jocund company.
I gazed and gazed but little thought
What wealth that show to me had brought;

For oft when on my couch I lie
In vacant or in pensive mood,
They flash upon that inward eye
Which is the bliss of solitude;
And then my heart with pleasure fills
And dances with the daffodils.

It Is a Beauteous Evening

It is a beauteous evening, calm and free;
The holy time is quiet as a nun
Breathless with adoration; the broad sun
Is sinking down in his tranquillity;
The gentleness of heaven broods o'er the sea.
Listen! the mighty Being is awake
And doth with his eternal motion make
A sound like thunder, everlastingly.
Dear child! dear girl! that walkest with me here,
If thou appear untouched by solemn thought,
Thy nature is not therefore less divine.
Thou liest in Abraham's bosom all the year
And worship'st at the temple's inner shrine,
God being with thee when we know it not.

AMERICA

America, you sparkle in the sun,
A paradise
Our forefathers sought and found.
With justice in your power,
With hope and love
You send your echoes far and hold a light
That worlds shall see and feel that liberty
And brotherhood are one.

For you, we live
And pledge ourselves to stand undivided.
You are a freeman's choice, America.
Yesterday, our fathers';
Ours today;
Our spirits in unison
Look forward.
America, you sparkle in the sun.

Grace Gladman Orme

BELIEVE IN AMERICA

Believe in America—her wisdom and her truth,
Her ever-reaching progress and her ever-searching youth,
The ills she strives to conquer and her aim for all things good,
Her promise of tomorrow for a stronger brotherhood.

Believe in America and help each new year find
A fortress for her freedoms and more love for all mankind;
Show zeal to meet the challenges and make all doubting cease
To sanction every effort for a bright new land of peace!

Frieda Jo Hawes

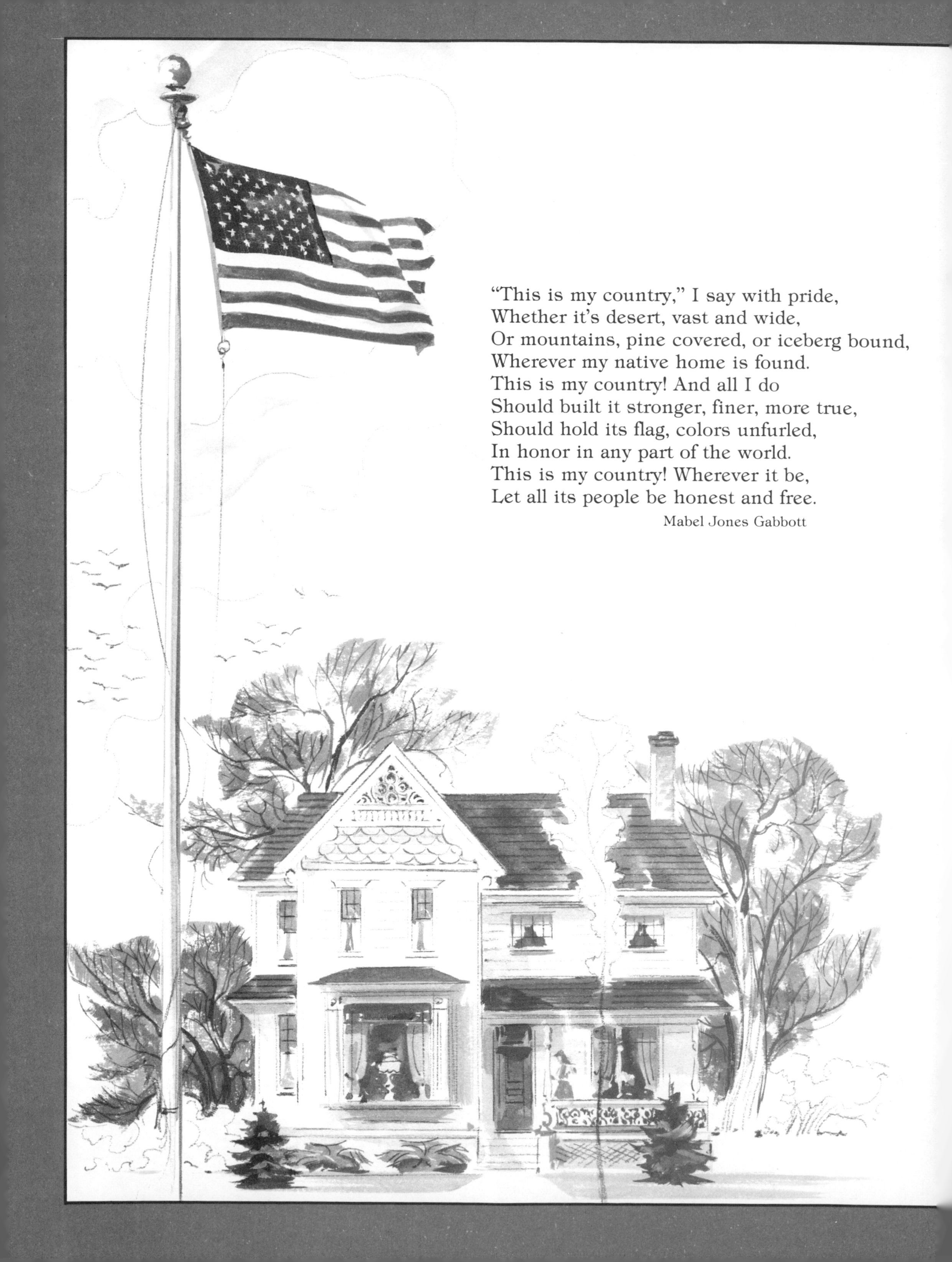

"This is my country," I say with pride,
Whether it's desert, vast and wide,
Or mountains, pine covered, or iceberg bound,
Wherever my native home is found.
This is my country! And all I do
Should built it stronger, finer, more true,
Should hold its flag, colors unfurled,
In honor in any part of the world.
This is my country! Wherever it be,
Let all its people be honest and free.

Mabel Jones Gabbott

☆ This Land and Flag ☆

What is the love of country for which our flag stands? Maybe it begins with love of the land itself. It is the fog rolling in with the tide at Eastport or through the Golden Gate and among the towers of San Francisco. It is the sun coming up behind the White Mountains, over the Green, throwing a shining glory on Lake Champlain and above the Adirondacks. It is the storied Mississippi rolling swift and muddy past St. Louis, rolling past Cairo, pouring down past the levees of New Orleans. It is lazy noontide in the pines of Carolina; it is a sea of wheat rippling in western Kansas; it is the San Francisco peaks far north across the glowing nakedness of Arizona; it is the Grand Canyon and a little trout stream coming down out of a New England ridge.

It is men at work. It is the storm-tossed fishermen coming into Gloucester and Provincetown and Astoria. It is the farmer riding his great machine in the dust of harvest, the dairyman going to the barn before sunrise, the lineman mending the broken wire, the miner drilling for the blast. It is the servants of fire in the murky splendor of Pittsburgh between the Allegheny and the Monongahela, the trucks rumbling through the night, the locomotive engineer bringing the train in on time, the pilot in the clouds, the riveter running along the beam a hundred feet in air. It is the clerk in the office, the housewife doing the dishes and sending the children off to school. It is the teacher, doctor, and parson tending and helping body and soul, for small reward.

It is stories told. It is the Pilgrims dying in their first dreadful winter. It is the minuteman standing his ground at Concord Bridge and dying there. It is the army in rags, sick, freezing, starving at Valley Forge. It is the wagons and the men on foot going westward over Cumberland Gap, floating down the great rivers, rolling over the great plains. It is the settler hacking fiercely at the primeval forest on his own new lands. It is Thoreau at Walden Pond, Lincoln at Cooper Union, and Lee riding home from Appomattox. It is corruption and disgrace, answered always by men who would not let the flag lie in the dust, who have stood up in every generation to fight for the old ideals and the old rights, at risk of ruin or of life itself.

It is the great multitude of people on pilgrimage, common and ordinary people, charged with the usual human failings yet filled with such a hope as never caught the imaginations and the hearts of any nation on earth before: the hope of liberty, the hope of justice, the hope of a land in which a man can stand straight, without fear, without rancor.

The land and the people and the flag—the land a continent, the people of every race, the flag a symbol of what humanity may aspire to when the wars are over and the barriers are down; to these each generation must be dedicated and consecrated anew to defend with life itself if need be, but above all in friendliness, in hope, in courage, to live for.

Author Unknown

What Makes America?

What makes America wondrous and grand?
The smile of a child and a kind helping hand,
The soft glow of summer beneath a blue sky,
A moon round and golden as evening draws nigh.

What makes America lasting and real?
A hope and a faith and a dream that's ideal,
A land filled with wonders, a mountain, a stream,
A nation of people with courage supreme.

What makes America? Living and zest,
Baseball and football, the dearest and best,
A freedom unequaled wherever you go,
Our dream for the future, to live and to grow.

What makes America? So many things—
A brighter tomorrow that each dawning brings,
A peace and a love and a home bright and free,
These make America so dear to me.

Garnett Ann Schultz

Little Fellow

Oh, gay little fellow,
A-trudging along
The gray dusty highway
Where soft maples swing,
Heart full of summer
And whistling your song,
Memories of yesterday's
Sunshine you bring:

An old-fashioned garden,
A deep shadowed wildwood,
An orchard, a meadow,
A green winding lane,
Songs of the birds,
The sweet notes of childhood,
A stream willow-shaded,
The gold waving grain.

Oh, gay little fellow,
Come wander at twilight
Back to the land where
The yesterdays call,
Bring to my heart the sun
Of life's morning
Ere gray shadows gather
And night's darkness fall.

Orrin Alden DeMass

Quiet Lass

Summer is a quiet lass
Who wades in little streams
And listens to the wind through pines,
Lost in a world of dreams.
Her cheeks are round and rosy,
And her hair is pinned up high;
Her feet are bare and dusty;
There's contentment in her eye.

She loves the fertile pastures
Where the brown cows come to graze.
She fashions pinecones into dolls
In such delightful ways.
There is a homespun charm about
The little songs she sings;
Summer has a gentle heart
That loves the simple things.

Grace E. Easley

A Country Heart

Let me find a country trail,
A pathway through the trees
Amid the berries growing wild
And fragrance on the breeze.

Let me find a grove of birch
That nestles next to pine
Where sunlit leaves cascade the light
Until the meadows shine.

Let me hear a tumbling stream
Refreshing age-old stones
And wander through the rustling grass
That only nature owns.

A walk in any season's woods
Where gentle things survive
Can guide my inner paths of thought
And sing my heart alive.

Virginia Covey Boswell

Little park that I pass through,
I carry off a piece of you
Every morning hurrying down
To my workday in the town;
Carry you for country there
To make the city ways more fair.

Helen Hoyt

The Country Road to Yesteryear

The country road to yesteryear
Was crossed by creeks that sang,
And just beyond the meadow pond
A country-school bell rang.

The covered bridge was dark and cool,
But sun danced through the trees.
The wind was gentle as it drew
A picture with the breeze.

The split-rail fences ran along
To make the road seem gay,
And rock walls with the creeping moss
Were patched in green array.

Along the road to yesteryear
We laughed and danced in play,
And so to keep a childhood dream,
We walk it every day.

Laurie Dawson

A Summer Print

Green is the color
That young Spring sees;
Gold is left
As Autumn flees;
White is the color
Of Winter's hair,
And plaid, the print
That Summer wears.

Red,
The early morning sun;
Blue, the skies
Where white clouds run;
Yellow, the glads
Which bloom so gay;
The stones
In the bubbling brook are gray;
Even the brown
Furrowed earth imparts
A fresh, rich scent
As the plow departs.

Green is the grass,
An emerald hue;
Gold,
The drops of fresh moist dew;
White,
The paint to the fence applied
While orange tigers
Watch with pride.

Such a beautiful picture
Could not be had
If
God had not painted
The summer plaid.

Susan E. Austin

Flight

I like to fly in a clear blue sky
With little white clouds below
Like a basket of fluffy popcorn balls
In a leisurely drifting row.

The golden sun with a smile above
That is cheerful and warm and wide
Casts a polka-dot pattern of light and shade
On the changing countryside.
Broad fields of ripening yellow grain,
Green, growing rows of corn
Stretch out of sight like a checkerboard
In the glistening dew of dawn.

The silver river is just a thread
Meeting tree-lined creeks by scores,
All winding and creeping and lazily sweeping
Their pastel valley floors.
A webwork of highways and gravel roads
Dissolve in the mists afar
As we sail on through endless depth of blue
Like a twinkling, beautiful star.

Dan Hoover

The Midwest

My Midwest, you have hills and plains
With fertile fields and wide;
While cattle graze in pastures green,
Cool rivers flow beside.

How beautiful, how stately too,
Your forests reaching high,
Forever monuments of pride
To live and never die.

Your lakes, serenely bright and clear,
Are grand beyond compare;
And travelers who seek to rest,
Find peace and beauty there.

The Midwest where the sun shines warm
And gentle rains abound—
No better land, no better home
Can anywhere be found.

Alma Brown

Country Churches

The humble country churches, symbols of faith—
They lift their spires toward the sky
Above the old oak trees and fields of grain,
Their altars open to every passerby.

These little churches, knee-deep in wheat,
Stand bravely, rising from the sod,
Where humble people kneel and pray
And offer praise and thanks to God.

Gertrude Bryson Holman

Country Church

I think the nearest thing to peace
  That men will ever find
Lies sheltered in a country church
  Where faith and hope are shrined:
A charming, white, old-fashioned church
  Where pious elm trees nod,
Whose spire in humble eloquence
  Points silently toward God;

A church with weathered flagstone paths,
  Great oak doors opened wide,
And kindly folk to welcome guests
  When they set foot inside;
A church where men return the love
  Of Him who fills with grace
The hearts of those who help sustain
  The Shepherd's meeting place.

Brian F. King

Small Towns Are an Attitude

Craig E. Sathoff

Yes, small towns are an attitude
  Toward helping one another
Where each man finds a special joy
  In making glad the other.

A small town thrives on kindly words
  And kindly deeds to share.
The essence of each day is this:
  Capacity to care.

Yes, small towns are an attitude
  Toward loving simple things,
Like quilting bees and church bazaars
  And Christmas carolings.

A small town thrives on hayrack rides
  And programs in the park
And picnicking and school affairs
  And bonfires after dark.

The attitude is one of peace
  From deeply thankful hearts
Who saw the deeds that must be done
  And gladly did their part.

An Old-Fashioned Garden

I passed by an old-fashioned garden
Beside a small village street,
With its gay potpourri of colors,
Its fragrances spicy and sweet.

There were glads in a row, tall and regal,
Striped tiger lilies bronze and bold,
Pale cosmos and ragged bright asters,
White daisies with hearts of pure gold.

Zinnias flaunted gay gypsy clothes;
Marigolds spilled wealth by a canna bed.
A sunflower's face brightened one corner,
And salvia flared in fireman's red.

Petunias and phlox of pale orchid hue
Nodded by gaudy nasturtiums.
Red dahlias—also yellow, bronze, gold—
Vied for favor with spicy-sweet mums.

For charm that is real,
A spot that grows mem'ries,
An old-fashioned garden
Has a special appeal.

Lucile Waer

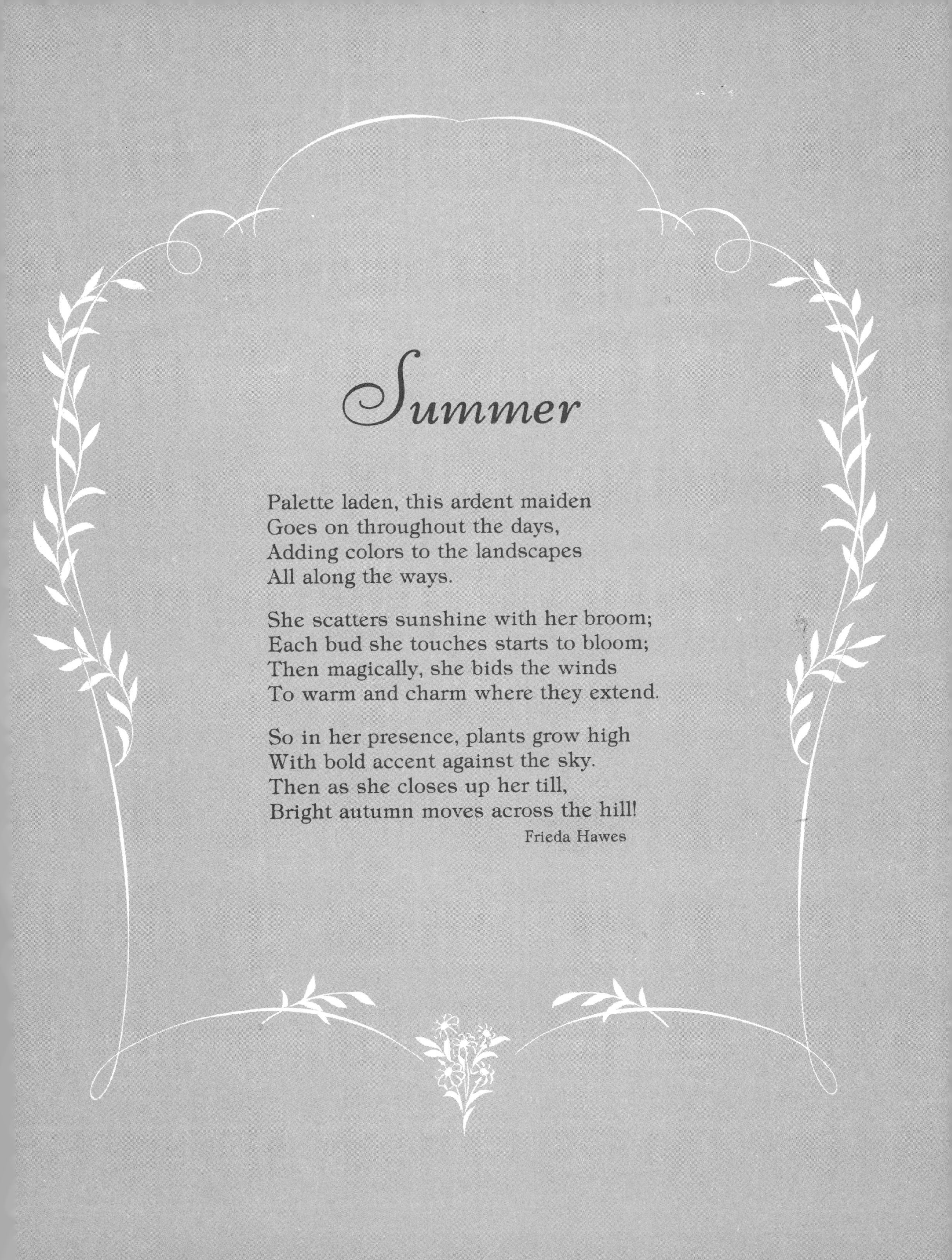

Summer

Palette laden, this ardent maiden
Goes on throughout the days,
Adding colors to the landscapes
All along the ways.

She scatters sunshine with her broom;
Each bud she touches starts to bloom;
Then magically, she bids the winds
To warm and charm where they extend.

So in her presence, plants grow high
With bold accent against the sky.
Then as she closes up her till,
Bright autumn moves across the hill!

Frieda Hawes

Harbor Hunger

I'm hungry for the harbor smell
And pungent winds blown from the sea;
The harbor holds much mystery
And secrets that she'll never tell.

The gray fog casts a mystic spell
About the ships, the boats, and me;
I'm hungry for the harbor smell
And pungent winds blown from the sea.

I hope some day that I may dwell
Where tankers dock with hemp and tea,
And white gulls circle wide and free
To tolling of a buoy bell;
I'm hungry for the harbor smell!

Bettie Payne Welles

America, Loved

America! From coast to coast,
What is there here I love the most?
The frenzied cities' bustling crowd—
The noisy tempo beating loud,
The quiet little town and glen
That takes you back to childhood when
You strolled along the country road
And watched the farmer's haying load,
A running brook to cool your toes,
And there in tangled mass, a rose ...
Then climbing to the crest of hill,
The view so vast you stand quite still,
The stretch of blue far out to sea,
A tiny island that could be
Another land, another dream.
America! You always seem
To have more beauty round a turn.
We really love you, and we yearn
For mountaintops with crest of snow
And wooded stream in moonlit glow.
But sight serene all beauty holds—
The stars and stripes in waving folds!

Barbara Moran

At the Seaside

When I was down beside the sea,
A wooden spade they gave to me
To dig the sandy shore.
My holes were empty like a cup.
In every hole the sea came up
Till it could come no more.

Robert Louis Stevenson

Sand

Sand, sand, sand
Blows everywhere,
Between our toes,
In our clothes,
Beneath the petals of a rose.

Sand, sand, sand
Flies through the air,
In our hair;
Everywhere
Is sand.
It steals
Through the house
On the toenails of a mouse
And hides between the sheets.
It creeps.

Vacuums buzz,
Brooms sweep,
But sand leaps
Into our shoes
And hides.
Summer flies,
And where's the sand?
Hiding in the attic fan,
Locked within the suitcase still
Until
Sand, sand, sand
Blows everywhere.

Antonia Bissell Laird

The Season of Summer

Summer's the season
Somewhere between
The wisdom of autumn
And folly of spring.

Water-splashed children,
A screened-in laugh,
Whine of fishing line,
Melons popped in half,
Whirring of lawn mowers,
July-fourth boom,
Music of night birds—
Summer's a tune!

Songs stored for winter,
Sweet memories to bring:
The season of summer
Which followed young spring.

June Masters Bacher

Homemade Ice Cream

Homemade ice cream is never old-fashioned. One of the best treats on any hot summer afternoon is a frosty dish piled high with rich, creamy, homemade ice cream. The summer ritual is dear to most of our childhood memories. It is not hard to recall the hand-cranked ice-cream freezer churning and clanking out the cooling treats on hot afternoons or the happy anticipation of licking the cream-laden dasher.

Ice cream making is too enduring to neglect. It is still a summer thrill to churn out the silky smooth ice cream in the shade of a sun-warmed back porch.

Interestingly, ice cream is not an American invention. It is a romantic world traveler with its precise origin unknown. However, homemade ice cream is an American invention thanks to a New Jersey hostess, Nancy Johnson. In 1846, she devised a crank-and-paddle, freezer-in-a-bucket machine that allowed the average homemaker to make the dessert with ease. The principle of ice cream making has not changed.

Most modern ice-cream freezers are electric powered; but hand-cranked models have been rescued from attics and dusted off and work as well today as they did a generation ago. Purists claim the best homemade ice cream is produced by churning a cream or custard-base mixture in a hand-cranked or electric ice-cream freezer, using ice and rock salt.

Ice cream is a favorite American dessert, if not a world favorite. Rich and creamy, it is a great treat as is. It is also delectable over, in, and under an appealing assortment of baked apples and pears, hot gingerbread, applesauce, spice or pound cakes, crushed berries, pies, fresh, frozen or canned fruits and sauces.

Darlene Kronschnabel

Countryside Tapestry

Special Thoughts About Summertime

The glorious lamp of heaven,
The radiant sun is Nature's eye.
Dryden

The curving road beckons the travelers on
As the view puts a spell over each;
With velvet green grass and misty clouds
Heaven seems within reach,
Mountainside inviting,
God's nature inspiring
The travelers—overwhelmed!
Stephanie Cook

Bright summer comes along the sky
And paints the glowing year;
Where'er we turn with raptured eye,
Her splendid tints appear.
Dr. J. H. Potts

The sun delights in bounty.
Under his smiling beams,
Plants germinate and mature,
And golden grains
Ripen unto the harvest.
Trees and vines
Spread out their branches,
And luscious fruits
Take on their luster
While ripening amid
Their settings of green.
Dr. J. H. Potts

Truly the light is sweet,
And a pleasant thing it is
For the eyes to behold the sun.
Solomon

Summer sun a carpet spreads,
Sidewalks white with heat,
All along the garden path
Patter of naked feet,

Happy children playing
Under swaying trees,
Mockingbirds a-singing
Midst the heat-curled leaves.

Thunderclouds hang lower,
Break, and shower rain;
Harvest days and clover,
July is here again.
Pidge Early

Sunshine is like love—
It makes everything shine
With its own beauty.

Author Unknown

It is a glorious privilege to live,
To know, to act, to listen,
To behold, to love, to look up
At the blue summer sky,
To see the sun sink slowly
Beyond the line of the horizon,
To watch the worlds
Come twinkling into view,
First one by one,
And the myriads that no man can count,
And lo!
The universe is white with them;
And you and I are here.

Marco Morrow

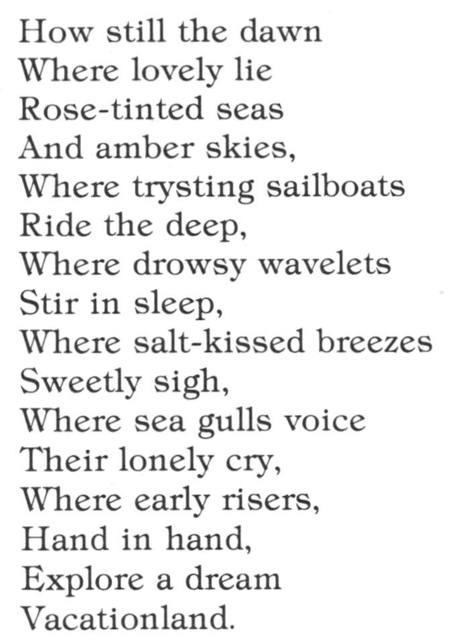

Go forth under the open sky, and list
To Nature's teaching.

William Cullen Bryant

July paints
A precious scene
Of azure sky
And forest green,
Of golden wheat
And scarlet rose,
A sparkling stream
That gently flows,
A fluffy kitten,
A dog at play;
She calls her picture
Summer Day.

Lois Anne Williams

How still the dawn
Where lovely lie
Rose-tinted seas
And amber skies,
Where trysting sailboats
Ride the deep,
Where drowsy wavelets
Stir in sleep,
Where salt-kissed breezes
Sweetly sigh,
Where sea gulls voice
Their lonely cry,
Where early risers,
Hand in hand,
Explore a dream
Vacationland.

Brian F King

When a man lives with God,
His voice shall be sweet
As the murmur of the brook
And the rustle of the corn.

Ralph Waldo Emerson

July
Is the green yawn
Of drowsing summer, all
Her planting done—calm interlude
Of rest.

Alice Mackenzie Swaim

Blue skies,
Warm winds,
Puffy clouds,
Myriad flowers,
Green grass,
Bare feet—
Summer!

Roxanne S. Smith

Mount Rainier

Mount Rainier! How I love thee;
Thy skies of azure blue
Are indeed a benediction
Softly watching over you,
And thy glorious snow-capped beauty
And thy pink and amber lights,
Lighting all thy rugged glory—
Thou glorious, wondrous sight.

And the pine trees and the shadows—
Ah, to me it's like a dream,
For my artist paints thee truly
Just like a fairy scene.
And the quiet, placid waters
Flow gently at thy feet,
Flowery banks of pink and yellow
Where the gentle waters meet.

Ah, my friend, thy God has blessed thee
With a talent rich and rare,
For thy hand has painted the glory
Of God's work—Mount Rainier.
And when I am a-weary
And tired sometimes, 'tis true
I feast my eyes on thy glory
And go forth, refreshed anew.

Mabel Reed Wilson

A model of the 70-acre 1982 World's Fair shows (from left to right across the top) the renovated L & N Railway Station with shops, offices, and restaurants; the Technology and Lifestyle Center with attached high-rise hotel and office complex; the globed Sunsphere (the World's Fair's theme structure); the 2,500-seat Tennessee State Amphitheater at the base of the Sunsphere; and the United States Pavilion. Extending across the lower portion of the model are other national pavilions.

Photo courtesy of The 1982 World's Fair

China will reassemble a portion of its Great Wall; from Hungary, Rubik will bring his cube; and 11 million sightseers will bring their imaginations to Knoxville, Tennessee, for six months this year starting May first. It will be the World's Fair, and it will turn the normally tranquil city of 180,000 into the world's energy center, in more ways than one. It will bring together representatives from countries all around the world and corporations across America as well as the visitors who will come to view the future in what is being billed as "the greatest show on earth."

Energy is the focus of the event, and seventy acres adjacent to Knoxville's Tennessee River will be covered with exhibits and demonstrations of the most recent advances in energy development. Among the nations which will present the trends of their research are Australia, Canada, West Germany, France, Italy, Japan, South Korea, Mexico, Saudi Arabia, Great Britain, Hungary, the People's Republic of China, and the ten-nation European Community. Australia is sending windmills, Saudi Arabia will exhibit a solar model, and the Japanese will bring robots that will do everything except take tickets.

Many U.S. corporations are set to have exhibits on the grounds. Sun Oil will explain the sun's role in providing energy. Federal Express will put together a $2 million laser sky show. Anheuser-Busch will bring along its Clydesdales to lead the daily parades.

Among the corporations that have become involved is a local one—Stokely-Van Camp, Inc. which originated in Newport, Tennessee. The company is now an international conglomerate based in Indianapolis, but it hasn't forgotten its roots. Over two acres at the riverfront fairground will be devoted to the Stokely-Van Camp Folklife Festival highlighted by three stages and continuous events depicting the life and culture of the southern Appalachians.

The most striking feature of the World's Fair will be the theme structure called the Sunsphere, a 266-foot elevated gold-tinted glass ball from which visitors will have the best view of the fair.

A generous sampling of all the fair has to offer should please the fairgoers. There will be entertainment as well as education. The list of performers is more overwhelming than the list of participating nations. Among others, you can see Red Skelton, Bob Hope, Bill Cosby, Chet Atkins, Johnny Cash, the Ink Spots, Carlos Montoya, Peter Nero, Rudolph Nureyev with the Boston Ballet, Roberta Peters, the Warsaw Philharmonic, the Kingston Trio, Victor Borge, the Grand Kubuki Theater of Japan, the London Symphony, the Dance Theater of Harlem, and the Scottish National Orchestra. There will be performances by 368 bands from all over the United States.

The six-story United States Pavilion will serve as an energy showcase. Sloping dramatically from the southern shore of the World's Fair lake, it will house exhibits of high-energy technology and strategies for future generations. After the World's Fair, the energy-efficient structure will become an energy research center.

Photo courtesy of The 1982 World's Fair

Associated with the fair will be sports events that include basketball, PGA golf, international baseball, and frisbee. The University of Tennessee's stadium which seats ninety-three thousand can accommodate much of this activity.

All that entertainment is bound to make anyone hungry, and the fair is ready for that, too. There will be fifty-two restaurants. The fare will include fast food, of course, and foreign specialties.

This fair is smaller in physical area than many other previous World's Fairs. Seventy acres is tiny compared to the 650 acres used in New York for the World's Fair in 1964. Other cities in the United States that have hosted earlier fairs are Spokane and Seattle (remember the space needle?).

The small area may help visitors who want to cover the grounds in less than a week. A spokesman for the fair has estimated that seeing everything once would take ten twelve-hour days.

The cost to attend the fair is $9.95 a day for adults, $9.25 for those over fifty-five, and $8.25 a day for children. There is no charge for children under four. A two-day ticket is $15.95 for everyone. A season pass is $85 until May first, when it will be $100. Admission includes everything except rides, some special performances, meals, and souvenirs.

The setting of the World's Fair in Knoxville holds another attraction for visitors. Knoxville is the gateway to the beautiful Smoky Mountains National Park, one of the best-known and most visited of the national parks.

Fair spokesmen suggest May or September as the best times to visit the fair. "The weather will be cooler, the crowds not as big, and the traffic not so bad," a spokesman said. Whenever people can attend, however, the residents of Knoxville are looking forward to seeing that they have a good time and happy memories of their visit to the 1982 World's Fair.

Dan Racine

Summer's Textured Weavings

Alice Leedy Mason

Come! weave a fine hanging
With summer in mind.
Use strong linen fibers—
The best you can find.
Thread the loom tightly;
Add nylon for strength.

Use a soft neutral color,
Some six feet in length.
Hand-wind a long shuttle
With mixed shades of green.
Weave a wide border
To set up our scene.

Show us a meadow,
Green dotted with gold.
Add daisies and violets—
A sight to behold!
Begin to climb mountains
Where a country road winds.

Fashion a rail fence
And tall northern pines.
Show pink lady's slippers,
A path leading up.
Crystal threads make clear springs
Round as a cup.

Go playfully onward
Where a saucy blue jay's
Back-talking a cardinal
Who gets in his way.
Green-up the pathway
With a thin, woodsy creek.

Add frisky chipmunks
Playing hide-and-go-seek.
Weave green for mountaintops;
Blue skies tell their worth.
Show God's summer blessings
Spread over the earth.

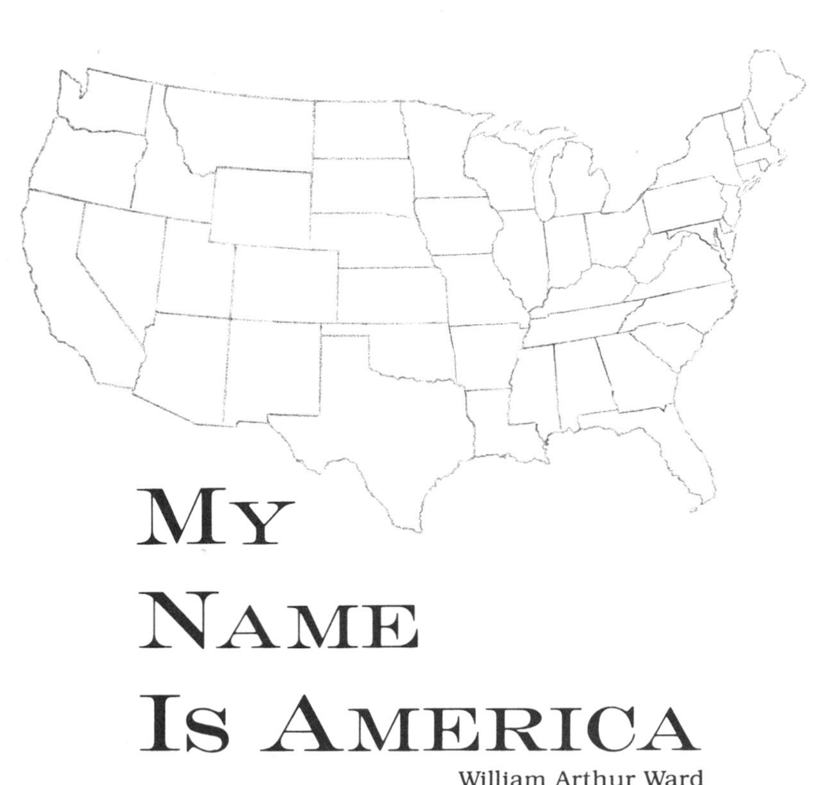

My Name Is America

William Arthur Ward

I am a country ...

but I am more than a country. I am over two hundred years old, but my mountains, forests, and rivers are ageless. Before I was a dream in the minds of mortal men, the land was a beautiful reality in the hands of a beneficent Creator.

I am a nation ...

but I am more than a nation. I am a republic of fifty sovereign states, each with its own heritage and individual greatness, each a vital part of one indivisible whole—the United States of America.

I am a government ...

but I am more than a government. I am a symbol of plenty, a model of representative government, a hallmark of freedom, justice, and independence to hundreds of millions throughout the world.

I am a melting pot ...

but I am more than a melting pot. I am a haven for the oppressed, a living adventure in brotherhood, a community of compassion, and a dynamic example of liberty under law, opportunity with responsibility, and democracy through equality.

My name is America!

Quiet Road

This is a quiet road where wheels have not
taken over completely. Though they pass along
now and then, it is like a song
evanescent and fleeting or a thought
rumbling wagonlike and comfortable.
Grass has time to grow between the sounds!

Dust settles, smooth and even. Sunlight pounds
down shadows of the leaves to chronicle
natures of trees and vines and plants. Old tracks
shrink cordially to make room for flowers.
Squirrels lie stretched out and sleep for hours
undisturbed. If this still road lacks
anything, it does not let us know
but closes itself in with many strings
of interlacing cobwebs, boughs, and wings,
with meanings that are indistinct and slow.

Helen Harrington

ALABAMA
CAMELLIA

ALASKA
FORGET ME NOT

ARIZONA
SAGUARA

ARKANSAS
APPLE BLOSSOM

CALIFORNIA
POPPY

COLORADO
COLUMBINE

CONNECTICUT
MOUNTAIN LAUREL

DELAWAR
PEACH BLOSSO

KENTUCKY
GOLDEN ROD

LOUISIANA
MAGNOLIA

MASSACHUSETTS
MAYFLOWER

MICHIGAN
APPLE BLOSSOM

MY AMERICA

Beatrice Drummond

NEBRASKA
GOLDEN ROD

NEVADA
SAGE BRUSH

NEW MEXICO
YUCCA

NEW YORK
WILD ROSE

OHIO
CARNATION

OKLAHOMA
MISTLETOE

OREGON
OREGON GRAPE

PENNSYLVANIA
MOUNTAIN LAUREL

RHODE ISLAND
VIOLET

S. CAROLINA
JESSAMINE

S. DAKOTA
PASQUE FLOWER

TENNESS
IRIS

FLORIDA
ORANGE BLOSSOM

GEORGIA
CHEROKEE ROSE

HAWAII
RED HIBISCUS

IDAHO
SYRINGA

ILLINOIS
VIOLET

INDIANA
PEONY

IOWA
WILD ROSE

KANSAS
SUN FLOWER

A place where I can freely visit wherever my feet would take me ... where I can go to the church of my choice to worship in my own way and learn of the One who created this wonderful, unique, mysterious world of ours ... a place where I can go and sit along a quiet stream and suddenly become a poet, for there are so many things in nature to inspire one's soul ... a place where I can study for a life's vocation of my own choosing ... and where we can choose our national leaders by voting.

My America ... where fields of waving grain ripen in the sun and await the time of harvest ... a place where rivers wind their way to the oceans ... where our giant jet planes leave their white trails across the heavens ... where trees don their autumn wardrobes of red, orange, yellow, and brown ... where I can walk in the woods and every tree becomes my friend because it provides shelter for me ... where the white waves dash our seashores and fling their spray to the winds ... where the canyons of the West change color constantly and where our national parks offer a place of relaxation to weary vacationers and travelers ... where a lone eagle soars from its nest in the lofty crags and becomes a national symbol exemplifying freedom and beauty.

Where the prairies once were roamed by the great buffalo herds ... where Indian scouts once stood their vigil in the midst of our great forests ... where canal boats once traveled the waterways with their cargoes ... where battles have been fought and recorded for future generations to read ... where the uniforms of our armed forces have earned respect, and those who view them stand a little taller and feel a certain mark of pride ... where pioneers in covered wagons once blazed a trail in their search for new homesteads ... where small towns turn into great cities with giant skyscrapers crowding the pathway of the clouds.

When I see Old Glory flying in the breeze, it brings a tear to my eye and a lump to my throat, because I know it represents my country and me. It is a symbol of freedom, beauty, and history. May God always keep it flying over this land that I call home, and may we always be one nation under God, indivisible, with liberty and justice for all!

MAINE
PINE CONE

MARYLAND
BLACK EYED SUSAN

MINNESOTA
LADY SLIPPER

MISSISSIPPI
MAGNOLIA

MISSOURI
HAWTHORNE

MONTANA
BITTER ROOT

NEW HAMPSHIRE
LILAC

NEW JERSEY
VIOLET

N. CAROLINA
DOGWOOD

N. DAKOTA
WILD ROSE

TEXAS
BLUE BONNET

UTAH
SEGO LILY

VERMONT
RED CLOVER

VIRGINIA
DOGWOOD

WASHINGTON
RHODODENDRON

W. VIRGINIA
RHODODENDRON

WISCONSIN
VIOLET

WYOMING
INDIAN PAINT BRUSH

The Garden of the Bells

At San Juan Capistrano, I paused upon my way
And lingered there a little space before the close of day.

And at the mission's gateway, I stopped and stood therein
To look upon the shadows of the things that once had been.

A wilderness of flowers, marigold and hollyhock,
Geranium and larkspur, the pink and purple stock

Flamed high against the sad gray walls and wove their living charm
About the place protectingly, that naught might do it harm.

And as I wandered onward, with magic all about,
A spirit led me to a nook the world had not found out:

A tiny, tiny garden set in a corner green
Of the old moldering courtyard, not easy to be seen.

Above the little doorway hung the image of a saint
With hand upraised in blessing, and carving old and quaint.

And a tiny fountain murmured with a silver tinkle there
Like the happy murmur of a soul too near to God for prayer;

Tall marguerites bent down around, and near its mossy brink
Green ferns were clustered as if they would of its waters drink.

Three ancient bells hung overhead, their voices silent now;
They seemed to listen as a bird sang on a leafy bough

That grew from out the ruined wall and golden blossoms bore.
My heart remembers all of it and tells it o'er and o'er!

And when the hurrying world goes by and I am hurrying too,
In the noisy city's tumult, there's a gate I may pass through.

A gate in memory's garden! How is it—who can tell—
That I stand entranced in silence in the Garden of the Bells.

Grace Bush

Stream Song

Softly and steadily, sparkling I flow
Between my mossy banks,
Cheering the daisies that gracefully grow
Nodding at me in ranks,

Winding through meadows of quiet allure
Over great glist'ning rocks,
Winking at clouds which high over me soar
Trailing their lacy frocks.

Breathless, silent, respectful I glide
Through mysterious woods,
Peeping at towering pines by my side,
Timeless, in somber mood.

Racing, excited, I joyously jaunt,
Hearing ecstatic call,
Dashing through dells to my favorite haunt—
Cascading waterfall!

Tumbling and sliding, haphazard I go,
Descend from breathless height;
Join in the glorious frolic below
Whirling in careless delight.

Puffing and panting I gayly advance,
Rippling a waltzing song;
Inviting small fishes to join in my dance,
Carefree I splash along.

Lillian D. Harriff

Nature Speaks

I know nature speaks,
For I have seen granite hills
Whose tall shadows lean across deep valleys
Where ferns and perfumed flowers grow.
And I have heard rippling streams sing
On their downward flow.
I've heard the birds twitter and sing
Upon the tallest limb,
And I have seen that same limb
Clothed in ermine, long and slim.
I've climbed to where the mountain laurel grows
Away upon the heights.
Eternal beauty's shining word
God alone can write.

Mrs. George Jetter

As unto a Shrine

As unto a shrine I came,
My heart bent low to Thee,
Eternal glory all about,
My soul content and free.
Dear God, so very close Thou art
Here in this stillness sweet;
No words have I to say in prayer
For this Thine altar meet.
But all the human heart can feel
And all the mind can know,
In adoration, Lord, I bring,
In thanks, in praise bend low.

Edna Greene Hines

Desert Magic

Sand and sand and dull peaks high,
Their jagged lines across the sky,
Thus the desert looks each day
To a traveler on his way.
But an artist's eye defines
Beauty in the roughhewn lines.

He can see in hollows deep,
Dusky shadows softly creep;
And where cliffs stand boldly out,
Sunlight playing all about;
On his vision, sunset prints
Coloring of many tints—
Brown and purple, rose and blue,
Shifting shades of every hue,
Striking colors that are found
Only on the desert ground.

Then when darkness shrouds the land
And night engulfs the sun-baked sand,
Fairy moonbeams weirdly dance,
The desert magic to enhance.
Over on some rocky wall,
Shapes loom up like figures tall;
A distant range of mountains seems
A caravan of moving teams;
Yet the silence is so deep,
All the world seems lost in sleep.

Agnes Davenport Bond

Redwood Magic

Step into a redwood grove where winds whisper of coolness and footsteps are drowned upon the deep sponge of earth. Find a trail and follow it. This is the land of the ever-living sequoia, and every step taken along its forest aisles will only enhance your appetite for more.

The light is muted; the undergrowth luxuriant. For thousands of years, cloud-sweeping branches have filtered both fog and sun, turning the grove into either a mysterious "other world" or sprinkling it with pinholes of light that momentarily outline the sword ferns or halo the bracken.

The earth beneath these auburn giants is a painter's palette of greens. Moss filigrees downed trees; maidenhair fern decorates decaying stumps. Trillium and oxalis carpet forest duff while the vinelike poison oak, in a seeming attempt to atone for its toxicity, spirals numberless redwood trunks and, in the process, graces unimagined heights.

Few wild things populate this climax forest, and the stillness here seems eerily unreal. It is an intense quiet broken only by the groan of branch rubbing against branch or the crack of a stepped-on twig or the intermittent scolding of the forest policeman, the bright-eyed Steller's jay.

This is God's own cathedral, far nobler and loftier than any ever built with human hands; and the silence here is such that even man speaks in whispers. For these are ancient sentinels connecting you by a hand-touch to all the centuries they have known.

This is a forest with a mood uniquely its own of peace, of strength, and of constancy. For as a race, these Ionic columns have survived the dinosaurs, the great Ice Age, and the forces that thrust the mighty Rockies skyward.

These trees will beckon, and you will find yourself returning again and again. It is a call triggered at odd moments and sometimes half a world away. It may begin with a scent. Or a sound. Or the way a lazy breeze brushes the back of your neck. Suddenly you are there, locked deep within the redwood magic, reveling in the awesome beauty of its dense, pure groves, touching a patriarch, inhaling pungent air, craning your neck trying to glimpse that special spot where treetops meld with heaven, understanding a bit more of patience and tenacity.

The flashback may only consume a moment,
but the spell lasts a lifetime.
There is no escape from the redwood magic.

This Land of Ours

Nadine Brothers Lybarger

I love the peaceful places of the earth,
Small cabins set beside its quiet streams
Where spring-filled woodland or the winter's hearth
Provide a setting for my fondest dreams.

I like farmhouses set on vast domain
Surrounded by green pastures in the spring
And in the autumn, swells of golden grain;
Such gifts of beauty all the seasons bring.

To see a stretch of desert where the sand
Lies, fold on fold, as far as eye can see—
Its massiveness, both elegant and grand—
Strikes vibrant chords within the heart of me.

I thrill to grandeur of the countryside,
Its winding rivers and its tall green hills,
A canyon precipice that opens wide
Revealing rocks where sparkling water spills.

I could go on and on. There seems no end
To thoughts like these from which thanksgiving pours
For countless gifts God has seen fit to send.
He's richly blessed us in this land of ours!

Beautiful America

Oh! beautiful America, land that I love
With great majestic mountains, towering above,
Mountains of grandeur, rugged and high,
Ever reaching upward to touch the sky.

Oh! wonderful America, land of my dreams
With beautiful rivers and sparkling streams,
Rivers of splendor, so deep and wide,
Ever flowing onward to the ocean's side.

Oh! glorious America, land I adore
With valleys and plains from shore to shore,
Valleys so fertile, so long and wide,
Ever reaching outward to the mountain's side.

Oh! marvelous America, land of the free
With people by the millions, like you and me,
People who believe in the God up above,
Ever going forward in the spirit of love.

C. T. Taylor

Canadian Trail

Wake me early in the morning, that I may meander through the meadow where morning glories smile and turn their faces east to the sunrise. The morning has covered the grass with droplets of dew that sparkle and quiver like jewels. Fluffy white chariots move quietly overhead, riding swiftly on the wings of the wind. The song of the meadowlark rings out clearly, breaking the silence of the new day. Nature is awakening with gladness, with sounds that soothe the mind and comfort the soul. I hear the hum of a thousand wings; I see the tiny hummingbird drinking of the sweet nectar from the wild honeysuckle. Its feathered body of iridescent colors beam in the sunlight; then with a wisp it vanishes from view. The winding brook ripples through the wilderness where no man dwells, its crystal waters flowing downward to find a resting place in the bosom of the sea. The creatures of the forest drink of it; their thirst is quenched, making them thankful. The moss carpet of green is soft beneath my feet; the rushing waterfall is music to my ears. The giant cypress trees rise above me like tall cathedrals reaching upward to the sky. The woodpecker drills into the cavity of a dead tree with vibrant sounds that echo through the swamp. The sleepy owl is disturbed and takes flight into the deepening shadows. The frisky squirrel squalls at me as if I were an intruder. The swamp has become dense and impenetrable; I cannot venture on. I am only man; the forest is not my dwelling place.

Wyatt Cullom

Cicadas Sing the Summer

Cicadas sing the summer
In August's grilling heat.
They have a certain cadence,
A funny little beat.

Pulsating and vibrating,
They sing the season's song,
The busy days of summer
Before the nights grow long.

They sing the time of dog days,
Of county fairs in town,
Of apple orchards ripening,
Of cornhusks turning brown.

It's back to school, my children;
Insistent is the call.
Cicadas sing the changes
Of summer into fall.

And when the fall has blackened
The vine with heavy rime,
We wonder where cicadas
Will spend their wintertime.

Minnie Klemme

Summer Fulfilled

Summer has fulfilled herself,
Still lovely yet;
She turns her face to Autumn
Without regret.

Her months are steeped in beauty!
Each blowing leaf,
Each fragile, dew-swept petal
Cups the belief

That Summer is the gayest
Of all the year!
And yet, with her departure
There comes no tear.

She makes a simple curtsy!
Then to retire
To usher in the Autumn
And its attire.

Summer has fulfilled her vows,
Though lovely yet;
She turns her face towards Autumn
Without regret!

Georgia B. Adams

Daybreak

Lorraine Ussher Babbitt

Time seeps through silence
As morning's gentle glory
Casts blue shadows
From the pinnacles.

Flush of first green
Lies close upon the slopes.
Rose awareness
Mists the mountainside
As patient power of waters
Chants from valleys deep
And echoes murmur
Their responsive litany.

ACKNOWLEDGMENTS

DESERT MAGIC by Agnes Davenport Bond. From her book: THE LURE OF THE OPEN AND OTHER RHYMES, Copyright © 1930 by Agnes Davenport Bond. GAY LITTLE FELLOW by Orrin Alden DeMass. From his book: DREAM SUMMER SONGS, Copyright © 1931 by Orrin Alden DeMass. SAND by Antonia Bissell Laird. From A QUIET VOICE, Copyright © 1970 by Antonia Bissell Laird. Published by Dorrance & Company. Our sincere thanks to the following authors whose addresses we were unable to locate: Helen Hoyt for ELLIS PARK; Mabel Reed Wilson for MOUNT RAINIER.

COLOR ART AND PHOTO CREDITS
(in order of appearance)

Front and back cover, Salano County, California, Ed Cooper; inside front and back cover, lupines and poppies, California, Alpha Photo Associates; Grain field and day lilies near Stone Mills, New York, Ed Cooper; Statue of Liberty, Robert Cushman Hayes; Little patriots, Robert Cushman Hayes; "Riverside Blooms," South Branch of Little Wolf near Waupaca, Wisconsin, Ken Dequaine; Covered bridge in Franconia Notch, New Hampshire, Fred Sieb; Colorful view of Mount Washington from Intervale, New Hampshire, Fred Sieb; "Fields of Gold" near Coon Valley, Wisconsin, Ken Dequaine; Cornfield near Hanksville, Utah, Ed Cooper; Church set in hills near East Corinth, Vermont, Fred Sieb; Gladiolus, Fred Sieb; Marine Gardens and Nubble Lighthouse at entrance to Fond du Lac Harbor off Lake Winnebago, Fond du Lac, Wisconsin, Ken Dequaine; Harbor town, Rockport Massachusetts, Fred Sieb; Coastline near Cape Anne, Massachusetts, Fred Sieb; Summertime treat, Colour Library International (USA) Limited; Heather from Plummer Peak, Mount Rainier, Washington, Ed Cooper; Eastern chipmunk, Rod Planck/Tom Stack & Associates; Remains of 115-year-old school, Morris; California bell, San Juan Capistrano Mission, California, Ed Cooper; Entrance to Bryce Canyon National Park through Red Canyon, southern Utah, Josef Muench; Mount San Jacinto and desert foliage, Riverside County, California, Ed Cooper; California rhododendron, Redwood National Park, Ed Cooper; Goat Beach, Sonoma Coast near Jenner, California, Ed Cooper; Kauai Honopu Falls and Na Pali wilderness coastline, Hawaii, Ed Cooper; Butchart Gardens, Vancouver Island, British Columbia, Canada, Ed Cooper; Yakima Park, Mount Rainier, Washington, H. Armstrong Roberts.

Autumn's Splendid Journey . . .

Come with us and take a journey down a quiet country road with the Autumn issue of IDEALS and enjoy the breathtaking splendor of the fall season. Our upcoming issue captures the color, texture and spirit of nature's most lavish season.

As always, brilliant color photography is featured, and you'll be further drawn into autumn's rich scenery through an outstanding selection of poetry and prose. Special themes include October hayrides, harvest reflections, peaceful walks in the changing countryside and Halloween memories.

Enjoy award-winning nature author Hal Borland as he writes of the stunning beauty of autumn leaves. Discover with us the whimsical tale of a determined acorn on its path to maturity. Also, share one family's exciting annual search for the perfect Halloween pumpkin. We know you will enjoy every page of our special tribute to the vibrant season of autumn.

Consider the joy you can give to loved ones and dear friends with a gift subscription to IDEALS, or treat yourself to a subscription of IDEALS and enjoy each issue year round.